GEMINI HOROSCOPE 2023

Your essential guide to love, money, happiness and using moon magic!

Hi guys,

A warm welcome to all my regular readers and a special hello to all new readers. I aim to provide a comprehensive insight into 2023 with spiritual, psychological insight, and down to earth common sense advice.

Every year when I write these books I just cannot believe how fast the year has gone, and that it's once again time to write and publish the series for the next year.

As many of you know, I've been producing these books since 2014, and boy has the world changed since then and 2023 will be a year of unprecedented change in world terms, that's why I've decided to also do an Astrology book of World predictions which include predictions for countries and certain leaders, because I feel that we need to be forwarded and for armed.

It's important to remember that no matter what is happening in the outside world, we all have our lives to live and karma to resolve and we must enjoy our own unique journey. Remember, we are all meant to be here at this very time, to experience what we are experiencing and we should never underestimate our own power and ability to thrive and make a difference.

Yes, we are all at different points along our own personal journey, but what I want to do with these books is encourage you all to understand your own creativity, power and never to underestimate yourself, to feel lost all to lose a sense of purpose. We are all here for a reason and we all have a valuable contribution to make in different ways, and hopefully my annual books have inspired you to understand your purpose and connect with some inspiration.

Fortunately the Saturn Square Uranus that was happening between Saturn in Aquarius and Uranus in Taurus is now done and dusted, which is a good thing because that was creating an enormous amount of tension within all of us, because the energies of Saturn and Uranus are so different. However, what we have coming this year is Pluto moving into Aquarius, and every time Pluto has changed signs there have been dramatic events worldwide that have changed history: it could be the birth of new countries, technological changes, conflict, economic shifts, innovations and the advent of new philosophies or political systems. So we should all be ready to embrace change with an open mind and we should remember not to be overly concerned with things that we are not able to change, because what we all can change is our attitude and it's always better to be optimistic and proactive.

I've often seen in my career as an astrologer that astrology works best for people who make plans, who act on those plans, who motivate themselves and who don't wait around for things to happen. Good things happen when we take chances, when we get up and seize opportunities or even just envisage then, very little happens we stick to comfort zones, resist change and hang onto the past for dear life, irrespective of the planets.

I always believe that it's important to understand our roots, to know where we come from and how our experiences have shaped us and given us wisdom. Our cumulative heritage is always important, but we can't live in the past, things are changing and we have to keep moving along and adapting, and using our wits and innate dynamic energy to thrive.

GEMINI HOROSCOPE 2023

Is this a good year for Gemini?

2023 is off to a really good start for Gemini, early in January Mars goes direct in Gemini which brings a lot of energy and impetus to your life, and this can help you to create opportunities in work and romance.

Mars in Gemini is an excellent transit for Gemini particularly because this year Mars is in Gemini for a long time, and thus it allows you to capitalize on the boost of assertiveness and decisiveness that Mars brings. As we all know, Gemini can sometimes be indecisive and conflict avoiding, but Mars brings a lot of courage and passion to your character and you're more able to take the bull by the horns as you feel a surge of personal power.

Jupiter in Aries is very supportive to both your social and aspirational needs and helps invigorate belief in yourself and your aims. There is renewed fire with respect to your hopes and dreams thus aspirations you have had on the back burner, without enough confidence to pursue, can now be brought forward and acted upon.

In general, social and professional opportunities are expanding for you this year, you're meeting lots of new people and travel may be on the cards. You are likely to expand in terms of your personal appeal and the reach you have, this means you will be meeting a lot more potential partners who are first friends, and as you know with Gemini, you like to make friends before you fall in loves, as this suits your perfectly.

Venus is spending quite a while in Leo this year because it is retrograde in Leo, this also favors romantic potential for Gemini as it brings out your excitable, playful nature, it also enhances romantic communications which serves to enhance your ability to attract love by internet dating and online. There's also the possibility for relationships that involve a little bit of travel or commuting, especially initially.

Gemini can sometimes be reserved about expressing yourself emotionally, however this year it's a lot easier to wear your heart on your sleeve, to open up to people in an emotional sense, and you're a lot more confident, which improves your ability to enter relationships that have a greater probability of being stable and successful.

The power of Mars to create

I spoke in the introduction about the fact that Mars goes direct in Gemini in early January, and will spend quite a few months in Gemini, this is a fantastic opportunity for Gemini to set your life alight with new activities. Usually Mars is only in a sign for a month and a half, but because of its lengthy stay in Gemini, it gives Gemini the opportunity to tap into all that fire power represented by Mars, and it helps you to be pioneering, entrepreneurial and more aggressive in pursuit of your needs and goals, including romantic goals.

The first half of the year is likely to be filled with activity, this activity is regarding your personal needs, wants and desires. Your desire level is heightened, as is your impatience, so you have a great desire to crack on and get things done. This is also very helpful in romance because you're likely to put the moves on and make a concerted attempt to get into a relationship, rather than delaying, making excuses, or being less committed in terms of making a relationship work.

This energy can be somewhat counterproductive in marriages because you will want to further your own interests and can be slightly more selfish. As you're a lot more assertive, you're less open-minded and less flexible than you usually are.

Making a splash

The opening months of the year are your opportunity to show the world what you can do, to make an impression and to get the ball rolling. It's an excellent time to get ventures off the ground, but like I say it's also a good time for you to make a stand in relationships. So for example, if you had felt your relationships were moving in the wrong direction or not fulfilling your needs, you have a lot of power right now to change the direction of relationship and thus to help you and your partner develop a more proactive stance in dealing with your life together.

You are fiercely independent and less likely to rely on others, you are slightly more bossy and you will want to force the issue when it comes to anything you feel strongly about.

Looking to break free

Your personality tends to be far more dominant this year, you're not necessarily desiring to have power or to control people, but you certainly want to control your own destiny and you don't want to follow rules or directives that you don't feel are authentic. Thus if you have been putting up and shutting up, it's far more likely that you will express frustration and will suddenly and impetuously end any activity that you don't have your heart in.

Take me on, Take on me

While you are not emotional in terms of being needy this year, the fiery side of your nature comes to the fore and emotions that are slightly more hot-headed, amorous and passionate unlock and are more in evident your approach to relationships especially.

You may take your partner by surprise, because Gemini is typically more cool, calm and level-headed and even a lot more avoidant, however this year you're more likely to take a direct approach as there's a sense of urgency to you, and you don't feel the need for your usual procrastination or coy way of approaching things. You are riding into battle looking to take things on head on.

Owning your power before it owns you

The more you are free to make your own decisions and to be the master of your destiny, the happier you are and the quicker you make progress. However, the more you're in a corner, are being dominated by others and are not free, the more you can experience frustration. You must deal with this in a positive way or else it can result in accidents, particularly to do with speed, or it can also result in illnesses to do with the heart or circulatory system.

It's very important for Gemini to lower cholesterol, to do regular exercise and improve your general heart health, especially from the beginning of the year. This is a wonderful year for new exercise, fitness routines and better dietary habits.

Your physical energy is very high and you should be able to achieve a lot of work, both physical and mental, but as I say you should be careful of accidents because you're not always concentrating or being present in the moment. You should adhere to the old adage, more haste less speed.

Relighting your inner fire

This is an important year for you to reignite your ideals and wishes for the future and often uniting with others and joining groups and organizations can be an important Launchpad for some of your ideas. It's of considerable benefit for your to network, seek likeminded people and expand your social circles, so you should be more involved with groups, organizations or even professional bodies which can help you to understand the potential of your life. You're likely to meet people who will enhance your life either through education or thought provoking romance.

No one is an island, and Gemini understands better than most people the importance of working with others and learning about yourself via interactions with others, and this year is a point in case. It's very important for you to motivate yourself by becoming involved in activities that enhances your aims, but which are also connected to wider societal goals or issues.

Friendships are gold

Friendships deepen this year and often friends are more supportive than usual, you will also make new friends who will become extremely valuable as allies, and as a gateway to new experiences including love.

Starting a fire

This is quite an impatient and also an idealistic time for Gemini, it's a time where you will want to start many new activities and it's almost like you're lighting quite a few fires, and these fires can get out of control. You have a lot of enthusiasm and your innate Gemini positivity is ignited, and this can help your make great progress including on your health and wellness.

Jupiter in Taurus conjunct the North node encourages you to understand limits and traditions

Jupiter will also be in Taurus this year in your solar 12th house and during this phase it will turn retrograde and contact the North node.

During the time in which Jupiter is retrograde in Taurus, it's necessary for you to stay within the boundaries of what is typical or conventional. This is a time when it's important for your to be conservative, now while your general mode this year is to be quite expansive, hopeful idealistic and optimistic, during the middle phases of the year, it's important for your to tie yourself down to some structure and routine. During this space, you have to take your innovative new approaches and begin to go deeper in understanding how this all ties in to certain sets of core beliefs and values of your own or societies.

Fulfilling expectations

It's important for Gemini to be cognizant of the fact that you have raised people's expectations, and you have set the bar for yourself quite high. You may not always realize how much people are relying on you, and looking to you for insight and inspiration, but during the middle of the year, you could feel quite a weight of responsibility to follow through and to do what is expected to you. This is a time when you actually become more thoughtful and reflective and understand the magnitude of what's really going on.

The midyear audit

While 2023 gets off to an extremely active and quite exciting start, the middle part of the year can be more of an internal process, one in which you require wisdom and begin to understand what's really going on in the dynamics of your relationship with your family, and also your work. So while you may appear to be spending a lot of time doing things that are outgoing and external, in the middle half of the year your internal development is quite significant and this is when you're more likely to become private and retreat a little, looking for reassurance from family.

Tradition and rites of passage hold key to enlightenment

One of the interesting things this year, is there may be a need for you to be involved in some kind of initiation or ceremony. You may have me to adopt some sort of tradition or become involved in a new type of custom or religion. It maybe a new relationship which awakens you to an interest in spirituality, and that new interest could involve some sort of structure: this could be attending mass; it could be learning to meditate; it could be going on retreats with a new partner where there is some sort of spiritual ceremony or initiation.

Your intense curiosity can lead you to many different places, and some of those places will involve something which is quite spiritual and you will want to explore the esoteric side of life to add a new dimension to your understanding.

While there is a great need to do new things and to explore, there's also a great need to understand what is going on at a far deeper level and the value of the esoteric becomes paramount in your search for truth.

Earning your stripes

During this year, you may engage in higher education or join an institution to pursue knowledge or to expand your skills. This is likely to be a year of increased studying and also learning through formal and informal mechanisms. Much of the learning achieved is through experience in group situations and of group dynamics.

As you are seeking guidance this year, it's highly likely that you will meet someone or speak to someone who can act as either a psychologist, a counsellor or an elder who can give your wise guidance.

Money flows where adrenaline goes

You are often very generous this year, you're not always good with money because you tend to spend it as quickly as it comes in. So while you're great at generating new opportunities, it might be a year of more outgoings than incomings, often because you are investing so much in your education, or promotion or funding new opportunities, and you don't always stop to count the cost, but knowing Gemini you have a plan, and you will be able to turn everything into money at some point in your own inimitable style.

Still Waters Deep Ground in Love

The spiritual element of relationships is very important to Gemini. This year new relationships will tend to have a slightly enhanced flavor in terms of the fact there is a cosmic connection. So this is a year when you can meet your soulmate or someone with whom you feel there is a special rapport and something that goes beyond the emotional and the physical. This makes it a very exciting year for relationships, but it can also be a little bit more complicated because these sort of spiritual relationships often involve a journey of self-discovery, and often it's rather revealing in terms of your own character and that of your partner, as karmic scars can be revealed.

Hard work improves solid gold relationship bonds

During this year existing relationships can become a lot more successful in very practical ways, as you and your partner may be able to work better together. Even if things have been difficult, being able to work together on practical problems could mean that you guys re-establish core respect and trust, this can help the relationship get back onto an even keel.

In relationships, it's very important that you are willing to meet your partner's needs and vice versa. That's why re-establishing balance is very important. If you have felt that the relationship had become unmanageable or you'd lost the plot, Mars can help your to re-establish some control. However, both you and your partner have to be willing to work at things and then a lot can be achieved. It's all about acknowledgement of where dissatisfaction stems from, where needs are not truly appreciated and then ploughing energy back into understanding and creating balance. It's a time to invest in relationships not run away from problems, make excuses or explain things away logically.

Marriage

This can be a transformative time in relationships, often relationships reach a crossroads and it's a case of having to adapt or fully reconsider the relationship. Good relationships can become a lot stronger this year with greater cooperation, emotional understanding and more awareness of each other's needs, but in relationships that are poor, the gap can grow a wider and things can become more bitter and you have to watch out for issues of control.

Gemini are generally looking for closer and more rewarding relationships and if that's not forthcoming you can sometimes become a little closed or evasive and this could lead to jealousy, so you do have to watch off for your partner becoming a green-eyed monster. You have to be patient in relationships because while it's possible to improve your relationships right now, this can't be done overnight and therefore a consistent sustained effort it is needed. Relationships this year need a lot of stamina, they can be demanding and exhausting and so some breaks and space are very important too.

Restoration and rehabilitation is a theme, if you feel your marriage could benefit from counselling or sex counselling you should definitely go for it, as things can be restored, but at the same time there are also sacrifices to be made and some compromises that are needed to save a relationship - this can be quite difficult.

You're not starry-eyed

While in new relationship the interest can be quite spiritual, you are not inclined to enter starry-eyed, rose colored glasses type relationships. It's very important for you to understand when going into a new romance what each of you expect of each other, and sometimes cyber or internet dating relationships can be helpful in this regard, simply because they incorporate extra time to discuss things as you get to know each other through written communication.

Gemini are at your emotional best when you establish a new connection with a person who is fairly stable and level-headed, someone who brings insight and perspective into your life, but at the same time someone who is very self-aware and grounded, because that is the ideal relationship within which you can establish a balance.

You may indeed get involved in a relationship where there is a considerable age difference and there may be an almost parent-teacher mother child dynamic to the relationship. In a positive sense a partner with experience can possibly teach you or guide you and provide an extra sense of stability or security that can aid your self-esteem, which in general is improving this year.

Love is a steady steam liner

In general your relationships have a degree of stability, but ultimately relationships will survive only if they take account of the real and authentic needs of you and your partner, and there is honesty, trust and integrity in the relationship. It's very important for Gemini to establish good communication, but communication based on honesty, rather than simply keeping the peace and smoothing over problems until another day.

Your surge of energy at the beginning of the year should be used to create some new rules of debate and some discussion, so that any fissures all flaws in the relationship can come to the fore and be dealt with. The aim this year is to create more balance and to bring more honesty into the relationship, so that needs are satisfied or the relationship is put under consideration.

The more real your relationship is, the better it will withstand any pressures this year, but there will be some pressures because you are more impatient and possibly a little less tolerant.

Getting Recognition

This is a year where your preparations begin bear fruit and this often coincides with an important promotion, success, recognition or culmination of activities. In many cases you are at the pinnacle of your professional life and there are often very important responsibilities and duties for you to carry out.

During this year you are more visible to the public, you may rise to social prominence, but at the same time when people's eyes are on your, you will be held to account and you will have to show integrity and to live up to a high standard, otherwise you can be subject to criticism.

While at this stage you can receive acclaim and reward, anything you have done which has been incomplete or ill-advised could cause your downfall. This is a time of karma which brings either reward or in some cases disgrace.

You have to be careful about what you do and how you are perceived in public. You may have less privacy and your private life can come under scrutiny.

Your relationship with authority figures becomes more important, and if you have a history of poor relationships with authority, or your parents, this is a period when you can iron that out and possibly change mind sets and patterns in this regard.

Love and Maturity

This is a period when relationships come into focus and you are required to grow in terms of your approach to and understanding of the role that you play in relationships and their evolvement

Both business and personal relationships need work and adaptation and so you have to increase your awareness of relationship dynamics.

This is a good time for a leap forward in your longer term relationships i.e. getting married or marriage counseling.

Your ability to negotiate or cooperate with others is important in terms of your success.

This is a time when you should work on your self-esteem and self-worth to improve confidence.

Creative Conflict

2023 can have a tricky start in terms of relationships because Gemini are less sensitive, probably because you're more self-directed and a little bit impatient in relationships. It's important for there to be give and take, and a little bit of creative conflict in love for the purpose of renewal.

If you have perceived the balance has shifted in the wrong direction, you will now grab the reins and want to seize power in relationships and that could rock the boat.

Good relationships can be reinvigorated by your increased desire and impetus to get things done and work on problems, but shaky relationships may become less secure simply because you are not always very co-operative and you don't necessarily want to yield to the demands of others. You could also be a lot more impatient with discussion and debate, and you could be more inclined to take things into your own hands without consulting your partner.

Juggling a dozen balls

Often your desire this year to become involved in activities that are expansive, involve other people or are politically motivated or aimed of the greater good can take your away from the family. So it seems that you are juggling many balls from the beginning of the year as you're initiating many new activities and it will take a lot of energy and commitment to keep them all going. So there are some times when you are forgetful and a little bit distracted, and your partner should not take that as an insult or a rejection, it's simply that you are throwing everything at this year and you don't always follow through on everything you start.

Ready to snap

Gemini are people who like to take your time in making decisions and considering different viewpoints, but the Martian energy makes you more impetuous, and therefore you are more likely to jump into something without thinking it through, but this certainly increases spontaneity, and may actually open some doors for you. You'll engage in relationships and activities that you wouldn't usually consider partly because you are more daring and even a little reckless.

Biding your time at work

In connection with work, Saturn is entering Pisces, thus the need to conform to an organizational culture and rules and boundaries are quite important. So if you are moving into a new profession or a new career, it is often very important for your to learn the ropes, understand the protocols and get a firm grip of the power structure in order to thrive long term.

As you're often involved in a new career this year, it's important for you to fit in with others, rather than trying to innovate or transform. So you must get your feet under the table and accept a certain degree of authority in the short-term, this is not the right time to be challenging the way things are done as there may be many unspoken rules that you need to be cognizant of. However, you will find that if you play the game, many people will be there to provide you with precious, ongoing support.

You could seek the advice from professionals: professional investment advisers or stockbrokers as because of the financial climate, there are loads of unknowns and it's wise to get more information.

Mentally it's an evolution or revolution

This year will lead to major changes in the way you think about prosperity, and your attitude to your possessions, your property or your income stream may change leading to new priorities.

Events in the outside world could propel your to place value on things which previously you would have disregarded or seen as unimportant or irrelevant to your life. This year is all about discovering a different way of living that generates meaning, many of the things you used to enjoy in the past can fall by the wayside and new things can enter your world which suddenly feel vitally important and very fulfilling.

The way you conduct relationships is also undergoing a metamorphosis. Within Geminis, at the moment, there is deep psychological change afoot, you are more self-aware and able to see yourself in an analytical way, and therefore your way of dealing with your problems changes. This can actually make you a better partner because you see the totality of events or issues in the relationship from a less subjective perspective.

Financial reshuffle

In terms of finances, there may be a temporary pause this year while you do a big readjustment. It may be that you are investing a new career and there is a period where cash flow is short, it could be starting a new business with large outgoings, or prompted by external events you could have a whole rethink about the way you earn money, and you may rearrange your affairs to be more resilient in the face of economic turbulence.

It's very important for you to become less materialistic, because the kind of savings plans, regular income streams or your corporate budget may be less achievable or certain, and a whole new attitude to money, things of value and financial priorities will have to be contemplated.

You are enormously resourceful in terms of earning money this year, and that will certainly stand you in good stead, you are at your best when your back is to the wall.

Communications are fierce and fearless

Gemini often has a reputation for being flippant and skimming the surface, but this year communications both with family and in relationships, take on a much more significant tone. You are more eager to get to the bottom of things, you are seeking psychological understanding and you're more willing to have in-depth conversations or even difficult conversations with friends, family and your partner.

Events will happen that will have the effect of making your much more aware of how your day-to-day actions affect others, or even trigger particular circumstances. You need to be incredibly aware of projection, as suddenly what you have been putting out there boomerangs back to your and you can no longer avoid it. This is a sign that although sometimes you avoid things, this year you are able to face things even if it's a part of an internal awareness process.

You are undergoing a period of deep psychological change, but this will help your to regenerate yourself emotionally, leading to a more robust nature and someone who is more able to deal with criticism and conflict.

Finding light on the dark side

In relationships, you're much more aware of the beliefs which you hold that are actually undermining your life, and that's why you're willing to re-evaluate your thinking and your priorities. In relationships, you're not taking anything for granted, loyalty and consistency are very important to you in love, and that's why you want to tackle any repressed psychological tensions that surface and no longer want to keep problems at bay.

A great need for security and reassurance this year means that you are able to focus on communication and understanding in love relationships in a way that you possibly didn't before. Your priorities shift for more to family and what is solid and lasting, and that's why you put a lot of effort into re-establishing good communication and understanding in love.

9-5

Your work life is very, very busy and it's essential to have a good work life balance, often you put in a lot of effort - partly because you're enjoying working with new colleagues and partly because you enjoy your work - but often you don't know when enough is enough, and you can burn yourself out. You have to be very careful that you have enough rest and relaxation.

If you are an employer, you have to understand people's natural limits, as while you are super enthusiastic, you shouldn't try and push people beyond what they can achieve, and at the same time you shouldn't have inflated expectations about what people can achieve, people aren't miracle workers.

Outsourcing is a good idea, but you should manage your expectations as with as everything in your work, often your enthusiasm is greater than the potentials of any project. So while there is a great lot of success and fulfilment within your work, it still may not meet your expectations which can be a little bit too high.

It may not be a good year to get a pet because you may underestimate the work involved and you have enough on your plate as it is.

It's important to have moderation in your diet, you should avoid excess carbohydrates particularly. In general your health is good and you can recover well from illnesses, but what can let you down is over work and lack of balance. So if you can keep a good balance, not do any extreme dieting or engage in sudden fads, your health should be robust, but if you are emotionally out of sync, if you don't have good boundaries with toxic people and if you don't get enough fresh air and respite from work and the demands of your clients, then your health could suffer.

The Messenger God

Mercury retrograde in Taurus conjunct Uranus at the eclipse in April indicates a time for Gemini to make a unique discovery or to be very successful in obscure fields. This is an excellent time for any Gemini doing journalism, independent research or investigation into corruption etc. because you could make stunning discoveries.

It's also possible that you may have to keep secrets during this phase, it's a very important to handle data, especially sensitive data with integrity. You may have access to client's information, or some information that is very volatile and you have to know how to keep a secret. Alternatively it may be that you discover something of a personal nature which you have to keep to yourself for some time, because you are concerned how people will react when they find out.

This is another period where you may interact more with the hidden elements of society, this could be people who are homeless, underprivileged or involved in criminality or drugs and you may be involved in studying aspects of these people or helping them in a charitable sense. However, you will be more aware of the underbelly of life, you'll become more aware of things that you normally ignore or are totally unaware of. This can be quite an eye opening time, and it will be both fascinating for you and also quite disturbing in some ways even though it's an interesting phase.

Home talk

Mercury is retrograde in earth signs this year, that's Taurus, Virgo and Capricorn, and this represents your 4th, 8th and 12th houses, the most private and personal areas of your life are thus affected.

In relation to your home, there may be a need for you and family members to backtrack on some of your plans or your attitudes. There may be unexpected events within your home, like unexpected guest or repairs that need to be made which could discombobulate you or cause your year to work out a little bit differently to expected.

You're more likely to want a retreat and have your home to yourself, so although Gemini are extremely sociable and love to entertain, this is a year when you are more likely to enjoy having your home to yourself and making it a peaceful environment, rather than having lots of people to stay.

So don't make this year when you plan huge amounts of dinner parties or having guests or family over.

In terms of home life and family relationships, it's important to interact honestly with others, to allow a full exchange of opinions and for everyone to remain flexible. It's often good to do things on the spur of the moment with family, rather than to over plan and over prepare.

Energies and Essence: Take it to the limit.

This month the key is grit, determination and showing your resolve. You are encouraged to think about where your boundaries are, and to stand firm on those. It's important to have a great deal of integrity and grace under fire, so while you should be diplomatic and not aggressive, it's also important not to be pushed around and to stand firm on your principles.

This is the time when you can win a lot of respect among the people who count, and also your enemies, by not backing down under fire and by holding the line.

Affirmation: "I know who I am and what I stand for and I embrace my power."

Love and Romance

This is an excellent month for developing new relationships. Cupid is ready to strike or has struck and you may well be dating a new beau. Love relationships this month are friendly, cheerful and loving. Affection is a key feature and you will spend time out, dining and seeing friends, and at home cuddling on the couch.

You are extremely curious and need a partner who opens up and enjoys chatting about themselves, relationships with Taurus, Leo, Gemini and Libra are favored. You want to learn a lot about your partner, but despite feeling that you are falling in love, you are actually revealing very little about yourself and that may become apparent to your new partner, and they may think you are just toying with them. You are a great listener right now, but you need to share too, or the promising relationship will stutter. Perhaps you are too cynical about love or scared to reveal yourself, those are issues you need to explore.

Career and Aspiration

You have to bite the bullet, you have to make firm plans and commit to them. Saturn demands new directions, but it's a slow birth, not a caesarian and so results may not come fast, but you should not be deterred as if you are strong and resolute, you can begin a significant new chapter that can result in a much more contented and secure lifestyle.

If things do not go as you have planned or are not going very well, you must examine yourself and ask if there are inner doubts which are bringing about this outer frustration. You should not be scared to ask yourself some fundamental questions about life, your past and your relationship to the past. How much is the past part of the present and is it over represented? Which of your values impact your life most right now and are you getting your priorities right? Getting to the heart of what you believe and how those beliefs govern your lifestyle is key to resolving the nagging questions and anxieties which plague you.

Excitement and Motivation

This an excellent time to set new plans in motion, gather information and look for others who will support your by convincing them of your arguments.

You may have to work out ways to overcome obstacles, creating inventive solutions so that you can achieve what you want and get where you want to be.

Positive change is on the cards and you may need to change your plans accordingly – so you have to be open minded.

You must remember to get enough sleep and fresh air as this is a mentally vigorous and busy time than can cause burnout if you don't look after yourself. However, it's an exciting and stimulating month, never a dull moment.

Marriage and Family

With the ruler of your solar 7th house entering Aries this represents a positive new phase in relationships, however there are certain challenges that have to be overcome, so the more codependent or need based the relationship is, the more you might feel threatened. The way to restore and heal relationships right now is through greater tolerance and through having a little bit of space mutually.

It's also important for you to be the one who takes the lead in relationships, don't just allow things to happen, don't be a victim of fate and don't be passive. It's time for you to initiate conversations, discussions and problem-solving in a positive and proactive fashion.

Positive affirmations that reinforce your ability to believe in your relationship and believe in your ability to restore the relationship are very important. In fact the power is in your hands in relationships, so don't underestimate the effect your own levels of positivity, vision and optimism for the relationship can have in healing.

Your marriage will have an unusual path and will probably defy the norm, its course will be hard to predict and it can have dramatic up and downs. You and your partner may not be able to depend on each other as much as you would both prefer as there are limits to what you can both offer each other due to circumstances. One or both of you may not want to be tied down, but may want something quite flexible this month.

Existing long term relationships may have to endure a period of transition while you and your partner both decide "what next" and I do mean both of you, as often with these transits one partner sees the other as the problem, and vice versa, and yet you both need to make changes as there is restlessness within you both. One may want more major changes than the other, but you both need more personal freedom and should not be living in each other's pockets or having a very restrictive, controlling relationship

Money and Finance

Your mindset is daring and imaginative, you have many ideas and are ready to stamp your personality on what you do.

This is a creative month where it's good for you to play around with new ideas or techniques. It's a time when you take a fresh look at financial matters and start tweaking, adjusting and upgrading and before you know it, you have revolutionized your methods and approaches and have found more efficient ways to manage income and increase your range of services and thus income streams.

It's an innovative time, it's a month to add more strings to your bow and be a little flamboyant. You will also have more fun making money.

It's important to allow yourself to explore every scenario and not to be a slave to routine.

Living and Loving to the Full

This month Gemini have great powers of perception and persuasion and you are able to strip away pretenses to get to the heart of the matter. Your romantic power comes from being strategic and rather penetrating in your thinking, you're quite skeptical and nothing escapes you, which is why you're more alert to underlying problems.

This is an awesome time for you to study psychology or deal with deep seated psychological issues or phobias, which prevent honesty and emotional expression in love.

You are able to tackle problems that have persisted over a long period and which need great resolve, courage and resourcefulness to solve.

Planetary Cautions

Mercury is retrograde in your eighth house. This poses difficulties for the household finances and if you're are married or share a bank account, there can be disagreements or discord about how and where money is spent. The retrograde period indicates that debt, taxes and issues about money are top of the agenda and often recent decisions have to be scrutinized or reassessed. It's also possible that you and your partner will blame each other for the outcome of recent financial decisions as there is a tendency to pass the buck until the dust settles and a plan is put in place.

All debt and loans must be very carefully considered.

Moon Magic

The new moon phase extends from the 21st of January to the 5th of February, this waxing phase is the perfect fortnight for new initiatives, setting plans, establishing goals, starting anything prospective and being proactive. This is the action phase, details below:

Mercury goes direct on 19th indicating that the communications sphere, financial negotiations, investment decisions, asset purchases, property deals and family related decisions can go ahead.

Sun Sextile Jupiter at the new moon favors short distance travel, education, exams, internet dating and IT problems.

Venus Conjunct Saturn indicates luck in borrowing money and tax affairs. This is also great for sexual relations and deeper understanding in relationships.

New romance is not favored nor are singles nights.

Mars goes direct in Gemini on the 13th bringing about momentum for leadership, entrepreneurship, negotiation, acting and sporting activities or competitive activities. Recuperate and improving health is favored.

Mercury goes direct on the 19th indicating that this is the time to really move ahead with financial negotiations, talking to the bank manager, joint ventures and even sex counselling.

FEBRUARY

Energies and Essence: "Looking for the light to find your place in this world."

This month you are drawn to subjects that relate to the community as a whole, anthropology and how people work together. As a Gemini you are a very social creature, but this month your focus is not just about making friends, being popular or establishing good contacts, it's more about understanding how you fit in and what your role in the world is. Very often Geminis drift from thing to another and you don't necessarily have a strong focus or sense of your unique destiny in life or how you can impact the world. Gemini tend to adapt and be flexible and that is where your strength lies, but this month you must think more about how you can be a leader, particularly a leader of ideas, and how you can use your wonderful communication skills to positively impact people in a wider sense than just your friends family and colleagues.

Affirmation: "I can be a force for good in many aspects of my life and I shouldn't underestimate the power of my positivity."

Love and Romance

It's important for Gemini to know who has your back and who respects your, you should listen to your instincts about potential lovers and even put your established friends and acquaintances under the microscope.

Romantic partners often won't say what they really think right now and so you have to work it out, however you must try to be perceptive not suspicious, as in February you have a penchant for glancing at the dark side of human nature and you need a balanced view. It's a bit like navigating along a dark road on a misty night as people in your life tend to be quite moody and emotionally volatile, you need to keep an even keel and not to get sucked into the negativity you encounter. You must be pragmatic about situations and while you should be secretly skeptical, you need to be outwardly objective. While the first part of the month tends to be dependent on the actions of others, or perhaps you have many obligations which distract you from your own needs and goals, from the 20th you should be able to focus on immediate concerns in romantic

29

relationships.

Career and Aspiration

You may be seeking out the company of artistic and creative people and could enjoy discussing abstract subjects, which can be very relaxing – you need to be with those who can stimulate your creativity and encourage that quirky artist inside you.

Gemini should use February to join new groups or clubs with a view to opening up social and creative opportunities. While you are putting forward your ideas with great zest and are trying to rally others to action, you will have to be more patient as others are listening but will be slower to adapt and pick up their tempo. Travel may well be an element of your work, especially if it involves dealing with cultural differences and is aimed at promoting better communication and trade relations.

Gemini may go on trade missions or travel to attend or to give motivational speeches or promote ideas for well-being.

Excitement and Motivation

February is a very exciting month of personal awakening and new opportunities. If you have been waiting for something to happen, or for the right time to make your move and reveal your true identity or purpose to the world, this is it.

This is a time when you are able the garner attention and have more influence over your life and destiny. This is a time for you to court adventure by being decisive and ambitious, and to grab life by the scruff of the neck and live it.

This is a wonderful period for renewal of hope and optimism about life's potential and you should give thanks and gratitude because this can help you to launch yourself or begin a significant new phase in your life.

Marriage and Family

This is a time of generosity in love, you are more secure and more giving, however you have to be careful not to smother your partner as you desire greater closeness and have a strong need for affection. You enjoy gifting and pampering your partner, you like to encourage romance and you are quite a planner when it comes to love and sex, you think ahead and earmark opportunities, then make the arrangements.

You have to be careful not to micromanage your love life as you can be quite controlling or domineering right now. You have very strong opinions and views about what you want and you are highly persuasive, but sometimes you put your partner under pressure and they may respond well initially, but this could create lingering resentment that precipitates conflict longer term.

Money and Finance

Gemini have to keep a beady eye on finances as anything you do now can have a much greater effect than you anticipate. Circumstances beyond your control in the wider economy can have a dramatic effect on your business, and so you have to hedge your bets and yet you also need to be flexible enough take advantage of anything that unexpectedly goes your way. You must ensure that when someone gives your their word, they back it up in some way i.e. with a deposit or written undertaking, as talk is cheap and you need assurances.

Living and Loving to the Full

In love and marriage, independent and headstrong attitudes can test your love relationships. However, it may be revealing to find out how supportive or unsupportive your partner is of your new ventures and aims, and this may reflect deeper attitudes prevalent in the relationship.

You should be patient and allow your partner to come to terms with any changes as a result of the things you are doing within your life – however, if he/she continues to resist and create obstacles, you may just have to ignore your partner's objections and press forward. Good relationships are mutually supportive, and in February relationships go through a phase where this assumption is tested – that is what is happening right now.

Your decisive nature can result in brinkmanship that could smash old boundaries and reservations and set the relationship free to enter a new chapter.

Planetary Cautions

PR and promotions are not favored and you should not launch a legal claim in this time or sue. Travel for pleasure, study and trade related negotiations are not favored.

It's not an easy month for your intellectual goals and often success replies on cooperation, diplomacy and emotional persuasion rather than the use of wisdom and knowledge.

It's an important month for good office relationships and you may hire new staff or indeed you may get on very well with a new colleague who greatly improves your attitude to work. It's important to respect the people you work with and not tread on their toes. You are more successful when you're inclusive and try to acknowledge the ideas of others, even though this tries your patience.

This month it's very important to be careful of who you put your trust in, we all want to have a hero and we all want to believe the best in people and sometimes we want to put our trust in people because we love what they represent and we feel it dovetails nicely with our ideals. However often these illusions are shattered when we put our trust in the wrong people, so this month whether it be your boss, a romantic partner or someone in the public domain, just be careful who you put your faith and trust in, who you listen to and who you believe in, because no man is infallible and everyone has their own prejudices and biases which influence their judgement and ultimately their behavior.

Moon Magic

The new moon phase extends from the 20th of February to the 7th of March, this waxing phase is the perfect fortnight for new initiatives, setting plans, establishing goals, starting anything prospective and being proactive. This is the action phase, details below:

This can also be the time for singles nights, dating and meeting new potential partners. Sporting activities and leisure pursuits are favored. A good period for dealing with children and young people for education, personal or business purposes.

Health and diet must be attended to. New diets may not be successful. It's not a good time to recruit or outsource. It's a time to be hands on in work.

MARCH

Energies and Essence: "It takes two baby, me and you."

The Essence this month is the joy of teamwork and sharing things in life, as everything seems that much sweeter when we have people to share it with, that could be a partner or a good friend, and so this month it's very important for you to nurture the most important relationships in your life.

Relationships are key, and if it comes between career, mates, entertainment or other activities you should priorities love and sharing.

Often we focus on career and aspiration and we spend a lot of time and money investing in these things, but this month I want to encourage you to invest in people and in relationships, and to learn to understand how important your loved ones are, whether it be your partner or your family members, and to invest time and emotion into those relationships.

Affirmation: "Together with others I have wisdom and strength."

Love and Romance

This is a fabulous time for love and romance, you are in an open and generous frame of mind and you feel comfortable in yourself and confident. Your marriage can improve with better understanding and more harmony.

This is an excellent time for dating and new relationships, you tend to have a good self-awareness in love, self-confidence and a strong self-esteem. You are likely to find a relationship where the other person will appreciate you and bring out the best in you emotionally, so it's a good time to embark on a new relationship or get serious if you're currently in the friend zone with someone.

During this month, it's important for Gemini to enjoy yourself and make time for leisure and fun. It's a good time to strengthen bonds with colleagues and with people who have similar interests to yourself.

This is a period of opportunity in love or dating as you are filled with ideas and you're incredibly positive. Even if there are other challenging ongoing situations, the energies this month help you to get support in love and experience optimism and calm in relationships.

Career and Aspiration

This is a time when things are very confusing, nothing is black and white and it's hard to find answers. You may be inclined to tell white lies and others may be less than transparent with you too, and so you have to make sure what the facts really are.

This may not be a good time for financial negotiations as there are too many unknowns and too much ambivalence among the parties.

This is not a great time for legal and financial dealings or analysis. It's good to stay flexible and keep an open mind. You may need to pivot and go back against a recent decision, because circumstances have changed.

This can be a time where you need a total break from your current work and employment, you may need to step away from the office, from the hubbub and have some time to think. It's very important for you to assess your whole attitude to your career, your life direction and what you are doing. If you suffer a big disappointment or something doesn't work out as you expected right now, this is definitely a clue that you have misplaced your priorities or have not been working towards something that is truly in line with your higher purpose. So it's quite important for you to be less attached to what you are doing, you are not your career, you are bigger than that and more than that, and if you have lost yourself and your true identity through trying to fit into the rat race, then maybe it's time to rethink your whole strategy.

Excitement and Motivation

This is a very lucky period because of the position of Venus and Jupiter in Aries which is associated with abundance, benevolence and good fortune. This is a great time for you to be outgoing, intrepid and adventurous in your life, to start a new romantic venture or to grab a new business opportunity. You should think big and bold, be competitive and express yourself fearlessly.

This month favors activities involving education, self-expression, personal development, publishing and travel. This is a fun time for taking the trip of a lifetime, for getting married and also for promotional and advertising activities.

Sudden help or benevolence from friends can make a big difference to your life.

Marriage and Family

This month the Jupiter Venus conjunction in Aries is a wonderful boost as it encourages your optimistic, adventurous and expansive nature. This is a time of healing, forgiveness and personal growth. You may feel a release of pressure, you are more likely to get emotional or financial support from others and that can help you deal with marital issues with greater confidence and control.

Because you feel secure and supported, you are able to reach higher and achieve quite awesome goals which bring credit to your family. This can be a period of important developments in your life that create opportunities for love to become more meaningful and satisfying.

This is certainly a time to embrace new ideas and possibilities and take every opportunity to refresh your life.

This is good month for you to get married or arrange an engagement or anniversary party. Gemini feel romantic and are inspired by the highest ideals in love, you are forgiving and tolerant and are likely to view your partner in a favorable way as you have a more spiritual outlook in love, and want to overlook what is either trivial or mundane, and sense behind it the greater purpose. You are quite self-sacrificing in your marriage and are motivated by what you see as the greater good rather than selfish needs.

Money and Finance

You're quite spendthrift this month and more money is spent on entertaining, concerts and theatre. Social life is costly as you will be invited to more events or parties.

You are inclined to live for the day and can throw caution to the wind, some savings targets go out the window as priorities shift to fun over finance. This is a good month for new businesses involving entertainment, especially for children, and for selling toys and games. Money can also be made arranging one off events or parties.

Living and Loving to the Full

March is a great period for chilling with some prosecco or a hot chocolate in the garden or by the fire and enjoying the inclement March weather, depending on where you are. Extreme weather tends to excite Gemini romantically and so experiencing the great outdoors where you are more exposed to weather can make you feel sexy and romantic. Gemini are in a very romantic mood in March and are inspired by the higher, more spiritual aspects of love i.e. the willingness to sacrifice, seeing the person for what they are spiritually rather than materially, love despite the odds, love in the face of opposition. In many ways love is more exciting for Gemini when there is opposition or a sense that you are saving someone, or being saved. Sometimes your attitudes to love are not very practical, in fact you are not motivated by logic and reason when you meet new people, you are motivated by feeling and raw emotion.

Planetary Cautions

Extreme sports and water sports should be avoided.

Emotional fluctuations are your biggest health issue as your energy dissipates faster when you get angry or upset and emotional situations take it out of you, so you should avoid arguments and hostility. This month is one of creative change where you will have the inner resolve and also the tenacity to reform circumstances in your daily life that have become troublesome, time wasting, or intolerable. So, it's important that if you've put up with something for some time, now it's the month when you must put your foot down and say, "No more!

Moon Magic

The new moon phase extends from the 21st of March to the 6th of April this waxing phase is the perfect fortnight for new initiatives, setting plans, establishing goals, starting anything prospective and being proactive. This is the action phase, details below:

This is an excellent period for reinvigorating your hopes and dreams and being inspired by life again. Networking and group orientated goals are favored. This is also an excellent time for innovation.

New career moves, job interviews and career changes are not favored. Not a good time for job interviews and PR.

Good for financial activities, acquiring loans and organizing tax affairs.

Deeper understanding and important discussions in love are favored.

APRIL

Essence and Energies: Succumb to your wild side.

You should act spontaneously and on a whim and may take off in an entirely new direction without warning. This can be a very good thing and rather liberating.

Often doing something entirely new or which is out of character, can help break deadlock and free your imagination. Sometimes doing something a little wild or even childish releases the spirit of creation. This is a time of celebration, and there should be events to attend and a chance to let your hair down.

It's important to do enjoyable things with friends and it's exciting to travel with friends or colleagues for both work and pleasure.

Affirmation: "I am more than my obligations and commitments, I am a free spirit."

Love and Romance

Gemini can be quite suspicious this month, you are careful about what you say particularly in love, because you often believe that what you say may be held against your, thus in your relationships, you're less forthcoming and you may avoid conversations about your past or other issues.

You are in quite a self-protective mode and especially with Mercury retrograde in Taurus in your solar 12th house, you may be lessening the level of interaction in new relationships, so you may ignore texts, calls etc. and just prefer to take a little bit of a step back and to think about exactly what has been going on recently in the relationship.

You're quite scattered in terms of your thinking and can also be very forgetful, so if you do not contact a new partner, nothing too much should be read into it because you're probably highly distracted.

You're also in a cool frame of mind, you are not feeling as in need of physical closeness and affection, that's why relationships can seem to stutter along.

Career and Aspiration

This can be a very successful month, you are highly self-motivated and driven but sometimes you try to shove your values down other people's throats which doesn't always go off well.

You should bear in mind the saying, "too much of a good thing," as at times something that seems like a good idea should only be attempted in small doses in short-run, rather than going the whole hog immediately.

It's important to have a balance between the old and new in your life, as while you are opening doors, you don't want to abandon old projects, old relationships and old commitments as these should be honored. There's a temptation right now to keep moving forward and put anything irrelevant to the new adventure to the side, however you can end up burning bridges. It's very important this month for you to pay attention to the clients, customers or associates who have proved loyal in the past, because loyalty matters.

Fun and Adventure

This is a time when Gemini can have a great deal of pleasure with other people, when you join together to achieve something of significance.

You can also have fun attending large-scale sporting events, big concerts or any event where you can get swept away in the vibe along with a crowd of other people.

You will be distracted by the lighter side of life this month, and so if you have anything labor intensive or laborious to do, you will probably not get very far with it. However, if you are working with people or in any career where being entertaining and creative helps, i.e., teaching, the arts, presenting, fashion etc. you will express yourself with flair and gain more attention. A positive month for self-expression and for working on or promoting anything you feel is a part of you and an extension of yourself –

so this bodes well for work you have a personal connection with.

Luck and fortune can come in unexpected ways, it may be a sudden opportunity from an entirely unexpected source which enables you to do something rather adventurous. This will often involve a large group of people, friends or fellow professionals, because it could be work-related, and there may be an opportunity to achieve something that will bring credit to your socially.

Marriage and Family

This can be an interesting time in terms of boundaries in relationships. You're likely to test the boundaries, to find out exactly where they lie. If you have a partner who is extremely easy going or adaptable, that partner may find themselves on the back foot or a disadvantage this month. However, if you have a more headstrong, assertive partner, you may lock horns simply because at a psychological level you are definitely trying to seek understanding of your needs and gain more satisfaction from the relationship. Some partners will be amenable to that, but other partners may feel that you are being a little bit pushy or self-centered.

Internally Geminis are suffering a lot of self-doubt, you really question yourself this month, so you need a lot of reassurance, but also firmness from a partner. As you feel insecure, a partner who delivers strong boundaries, clear messages and who doesn't crowd you will be very successful and this will help the relationship to become more authentic. Alternatively, a partner who shows neediness and a desire to control you will only drive you into silence and avoidance.

Money and Finance

With Mars in Cancer, you are highly acquisitive this month, you are also very driven at achieving targets. This is an excellent time to plough extra energy into finding new clients or increasing sales, however often you are more impulsive with expenditure, so it's important to make sure any business expenditure is warranted.

It's important for you to moderate waste and all assets should be working for you, and so anything from an old computer, fuel guzzling car or an inefficient accounting system, has to go by the wayside. Speed and efficiency equal money.

Spreading risk is important and you may want to work on projects with other people, simply to gain from their knowledge and expertise and also because they can share the financial burden of costs.

Living and Loving to the Full

Venus is entering Gemini this month, but at the same time Mercury is going retrograde in Taurus, this can mean that the way to proceed in love is through fun, light-hearted and playful social activities. You spontaneity and to be surprised, and you want everything in your love life to be thoroughly unplanned and uncontrolled. So the key this month for success in love, is going with the moment and not making plans.

The thing about Gemini this month, is if you overthink anything you can begin to have second thoughts or cold feet, whereas if you do something totally spontaneously you tend to feel more confident and to enjoy yourself more. Thus set dates and planning are out the window, you and your partner should take the month as it comes.

This a great month for Geminis and your partner to go out with friends, in groups or to leisure events, rather than having very intensive dates with a lot of conversation.

Planetary Cautions

Mercury goes retrograde on the 21st of the month in Taurus while squaring Uranus.

This month you need to keep your head about your and not to be caught in idealistic dreams or fantasies, it's quite easy to hang on to illusions but you need a cold light of day appraisal.

You should be slightly suspicious of people and their motivations, this is not a good time to enter any schemes that are highly speculative. It's also not a good time for you to dabble in the occult or to attempt anything in the spiritual realm, because you can easily be misled or mesmerized by people who have dubious intentions.

This time is a time of reflection and it's quite a good idea that you go off by yourself to contemplate, and that can mean withdrawing and having periods of solitude, simply to recharge your batteries and to decrease stress.

This month it's important for you to be productive, but also to pace yourself, as you should not get into situations which are highly aggressive or likely to be very mentally taxing, because you're less able to deal with stress than you think.

Moon Magic

The new moon phase extends from the 20th of April to the 5th of May this waxing phase is the perfect fortnight for new initiatives, setting plans, establishing goals, starting anything prospective and being proactive. This is the action phase, details below:

Health and diet are very important in this phase. An excellent time to get to the bottom of and understand health issues better. A good time to turn health around. Stress management is very important. A good time for an overhaul or reorganization of your daily routine.

Mercury is retrograde Taurus from the 21st indicating caution in dealing with large corporations and bureaucracy. Paperwork and applications for planning permission can be delayed. Anything involving government will be very slow.

Energies and Essence: "What doesn't kill you makes you stronger Stand a little taller."

This can be an energy sapping month. You have a great deal of persistence and deep reserves of emotional energy, and this can help you endure storms and keep you focused. You are very single-minded and not in the mood to let things get on top of you, which means that no matter what, you will achieve this month, even though it will not come easily.

Your energy is high and yet can be hard to control as you tend to erupt, burst forward then retreat; you do not always judge the situation well as you get hot headed.

Affirmation: "Every time I face adversity I have an opportunity to gain experience and become more capable and resilient."

Love and Romance

This month the ruler of your solar seventh house, Jupiter is entering Taurus, but as it does so, it squares Pluto which brings a rather dramatic element to new relationships and love.

It is likely that an unusual and fated event can happen right now that can bring you into contact with a partner who can be a soulmate, or even a spiritual guide. It is highly likely that a rather rare and usual yet preordained relationship can occur. This is one of the best months for your meeting a new partner who can play a significant role in your life.

A new relationship that begins now often gets off to a rather bizarre start, there can be mixed signals, some doubt and even some intrigue or games, but that doesn't mean there isn't fantastic long-term potential.

So while you should tread carefully in a new relationship, you should keep your eyes and mind open because this is a significant time within your love life

Career and Aspiration

When mercury goes direct is an excellent time for you to set your mind onto new goals, you will be more inclined to focus and not to play games or be distracted. The second part of the month is excellent for analysis and is also favorable for any public speaking, job interviews or exams that have to be taken because you have good problem-solving ability and have great concentration.

This month you need to focus on the details that other people may miss. The key to success and getting ahead in your career, is to be more alert to what is subtle and nuanced. It's also very important for your to be highly sensitive when you communicate, because that can also give your an advantage. What I mean by being sensitive, is having a heightened awareness of people's opinions, ideas and expectations and then adapting your communication style so that these people feel included. It's a very important time for you to reach out to anyone who is disaffected or marginalized.

Fun and Adventure

In terms of fun and adventure, an excellent idea for this month is for you to become involved in a project to repair, restore or reboot something. This may be connected to a project that involves the whole community, it could be a project related to the environment or something that would enhance the lives of children in your neighborhood.

Giving back and also uniting with others to build something that is of lasting value, and which will provide joy, is a very exciting way for your to spend your this time.

Alternatively, you may get your adrenaline rush by trying to reform your own business or the institution or cooperation within which you work, to encourage greater equality, diversity and inclusivity.

You enjoy projects that involve ideas, ideals and yet which don't involve any financial risk. Sometimes you like to use your wits and your ingenuity to make a difference to the people who you interact with most.

Marriage and Family

Gemini is more affectionate this month and you are more willing to give and receive in love relationships, which can become a lot more meaningful as long as there's honesty and trust.

You are slightly more sensitive this month, and you pick up on hidden signals which can mean that you are more responsive as a partner, and your nurturing and protective instincts are aroused. At the same time, you are still slightly more vulnerable, so this is not a good time in marriage to have any discussions that are likely to lead to conflict, simply because you are likely to be a little bit subjective and emotional.

Conversations about money and practical family matters may not get anywhere, it certainly is however a good month to start relating to each other in an affectionate and emotional or meaningful way once again. Tenderness becomes more important and you are quite loving.

Discretion is very important, as it is all about trust in May, so you and your partner should keep your secrets and not discuss the relationship with others.

Money and Finance

A certain amount of caution and conservatism is needed in financial affairs this month, this is not a good time for highly risky activities.

Reputation and organic growth are key to earning more money in your own business or getting a promotion.

This is a month when previous work done for clients and good relationships established tend to lead to good recommendations, good feedback or a positive approval rating, which can all increase chance of gaining a promotion or winning bigger and better clients.

Client and corporate entertainment is likely to be very successful, and you may run events from your home to improve relationships with your teams and colleagues.

Living and Loving to the Full

This month's love magic can be enhanced by spending quiet, intimate, private moments together, but these should not be slushy or sentimental, they should rather be an opportunity to share things and express fantasies to each other.

Often brainstorming new sexual ideas or even talking about exciting things that you could do together in the upcoming summer months is a great way to bond and get excitement back into the love relationship.

So whatever is going on in your lives, in terms of your intimate life you should let your imagination run free and feel able to discuss all your wildest fantasies and aspirations for the coming months with each other, and be bold enough think about what's possible rather than what's not.

Planetary Cautions

Mercury is retrograde in Taurus until the 15th of the month meaning that you should avoid dealing with large corporations or any humanitarian or charitable pursuits

During this time it's also best for you to avoid dabbling in anything very idealistic or vaguely defined, you need to stick with what you know and rely on facts, because this is a time when your intuition can lead your astray. Your instincts may be slightly off simply because you are more likely to err on the side of suspicion and self-doubt, and this can lead to a little bit of pessimism.

Moon Magic

The new moon phase extends from the 19th of May to the 3rd of June this waxing phase is the perfect fortnight for new initiatives, setting plans, establishing goals, starting anything prospective and being proactive. This is the action phase, details below:

This new moon period favors international travel and trade. Academic pursuits, publishing and learning are favored. It's a good time for social and community projects.

Marriage and engagement are not favored at this time.

Cooperation, mediation and new business deals are not favored.

Caution is needed in leadership and financial matters.

Political and organizational goals are successful. A good time for innovation.

Dealing with tax or audit issues is favored. A good time for money reorganization.

*Energies and Essence: "No longer ridin' on the merry-go-round
I just had to let it go."*

*This month the key is great awareness, using intuition and sensing what is
subtle and unseen. It's important for you to use your emotional intelligence
and your ability to perceive things at a deeper level. You are much more
sensitive to other people and tend to know how they feel intuitively, you
more concerned about others around you and you are in a highly
charitable altruistic frame of mind.*

*It's important for you to connect with others at a deeper level and to
experience life emotionally, in terms of sharing with others as this
increases meaning, however the one warning is you must be careful to
maintain some boundaries, because certain relationships with people can
become toxic if their emotions are allowed to impede on yours. So while
you are in a very helpful mood, you must remember other people's
problems are not your own.*

*Affirmation: "My awareness encompasses information and intuition and I
have the ability to perceive what is yet unknown."*

Love and Romance

Love life is again quite interesting and a source of great excitement, but
there is a complexity and very often you are perplexed by new partner,
leading to certain amount of confusion in new relationships.

Often in love you feel you're getting too deep, too quickly and you may
wonder what the hell you're getting into. However you're almost
compelled to go into new relationships, even if on the face of it they seem
crazy or rather complicated.

You're intrigued by emotionally complex people who are not quite what
they seem. You may be even attracted to someone older with a past, or
someone who is carrying baggage. You simply find complicated

relationships treasure troves of possibility, you are not deterred and will follow where your heart leads you. Usually Gemini think with their heads, but right now in love you're thinking with your passions and your heart, and you're inexplicably drawn to unusual situations in love despite yourself.

Career and Aspiration

This is a highly creative month, your creative juices and general love of life are in full force, you feel positive and are able to project in a really encouraging way to other people. The power of attraction and affirmations are supercharged.

This month is all about winning friends and influencing people, you are charming, persuasive and are able to wow people with your personality. This is a certainly a time where you feel self-confident, exuberant and it's an excellent time in business for making an impression, establishing new contacts or getting people excited about different ideas.

There is likely to be more business travel, but the business travel is likely to be highly sociable and enjoyable, there may be more social events in your work sphere or client entertainment.

This is an excellent month for public relations and improving your image, it may also be good time for revamping your website to make it a lot more snappy, jazzy and trendy.

Fun and Adventure

Intellectual challenges and debate really inspire you this month.

When you unite your new insights with your determination and guile this month, you're sure to make waves and get noticed. Nothing is as exciting to your as being heard and having your views accepted or acknowledged and you're able to get that this month.

Nothing much scares you off, when it comes to expressing your opinions and thoughts. You're likely to be excellent at what you do, and you go after your projects and will complete them with almost ruthless efficiency.

You're a little intimidating, but this may not be a very big concern to you, as you're taking advantage of your energy to go after what inspires you.

Whatever you have your sights on, you're going at it big time and life feels exciting.

Marriage and Family

This is an excellent time for marriage, there's more opportunity to host events and experience entertainment together, take fun trips and enjoy yourselves. The relationship is also working better in terms of practical communication.

This is an excellent month for achieving balance, understanding and consolidating in a relationship. It is a time when you are both level-headed and more able to see things in perspective, there is more common ground in relationships right now.

This is an excellent time for Gemini to achieve the real stability that you crave in your relationships, you find that your individual needs are less in conflict with the demands of the relationship. You are able to accept responsibility, but it doesn't feel as burdensome to you, even a slightly more traditional relationship won't feel entrapping because you understand the value that this has to you.

Relationships really define you and give you a sense of purpose, so it's a classic case of when people say 'my better half' as you will feel that you're enhanced by a good relationship, by the personality and achievements of your partner, and you are both encouraging and supportive to your each other and you feel supported in the relationship.

Things in marriage are fairly stable this month.

Money and Finance

The key to making money this month is in terms of understanding what's going on in society and understanding trends, new speak and fashions. You need to be reading a lot of literature or publications and it's very important for you to get through trade journals and newspapers this month to gather as much information as possible.

Good investing comes when you accumulate information from a variety of sources and then try to interpret the underlying trends that are flowing, and the direction in which things are moving. It can be quite a barrage of information this month, and therefore you are extremely busy, but being a very curious person, it should also feed your intense desire for knowledge and information.

You are in a unique position to understand what is going on at a more subtle level and take business advantage.

Living and Loving to the Full

The key to love magic this month is titillation, playfulness and trips away. It is important to take spontaneous journeys, even if they are just road trips where the destination itself is immaterial. Often travel brings out a romantic streak and you may feel particularly energized romantically if the two of you take a trip together, have a family outing or just do something silly on the spur of the moment.

It really is a case of the 'silly season', you need to forget your troubles and find a space where you and your partner can laugh, feel youthful once again and throw off all the cares of adult life. So little pockets of escapism within the business of the month, ignite passion.

Planetary Cautions

Gemini need to avoid any hasty, ill-considered communication, there are times this month where you can feel a little bit angry or frustrated, and you can say things or lose your temper in the heat of the moment. It's very important for you to bite your lip and count to ten, because often you don't realize the full consequence of something said in haste.

It's very important for you to analyze the ramifications of all your communications, you should also be extra careful to not send spam or over communicate with clients and customers. You are inclined to go a little bit overboard with the messaging, or even with the promotions this month, you have to be careful not to seem over eager or to bombard your clients and customers with either information or offers.

You have to be careful when being persuasive that you don't seem shallow or insincere.

Moon Magic

The new moon phase extends from the 18th of June to the 3rd of July this waxing phase is the perfect fortnight for new initiatives, setting plans, establishing goals, starting anything prospective and being proactive. This is the action phase, details below:

Caution is needed in personal and financial affairs. Gemini needs to be aware of being deceived. You should be wary of new business arrangements and unsolicited emails. You should be very careful of scams.

This is an important time to avoid anything dubious. Not a good time for charitable or humanitarian pursuits.

Not a good time for singles nights and new relationships.

Esoteric and spiritual goals are not favored.

International travel and trade isn't successful. Not a good period for higher education goals and publishing.

Networking goals and political objectives are successful. A good period for managing financial affairs of yourself and others. Accounting and tax matters are favored.

Energies and Essence: "From the mountains of faith, to a river so deep."

The Essence this month is being grounded, and developing a sense of stability and security from within.

It's important to develop an unshakable sense of calm and it's essential not to allow what is happening in the world, with your partner or your close circle, to shake you up or to destroy your own peace of mind. It's very important to have an awareness of who you are, what you stand for and your purpose, so that you have something to cling onto. They say that a tree with no roots will be blown over by the smallest wind, so right now it's important for you to focus on your roots, to understand what are the most important things in your life, and to find a grounded center in which you can face the storms that inevitably come this month.

During this month you have to balance a sense of feeling restricted, but also a sense of how the status quo can really help ground you and bring you back to a place of common sense.

Affirmation: "I am superior to stress, negative thoughts and base instincts."

Love and Romance

A chance meeting with a new potential partner this month can generate a lot of passion, your initial encounters with this person can bring out the best or the worst of you as your emotions are shaken and stirred unexpectedly.

Love and romantic relationships swing between the extremes, but if you can handle the intensity that they bring, a spiritual and rewarding partnership can emerge with long term potential. You must be ready however for this relationship to continue to have a few sharp edges to it, but this certainly piques your interest.

There are challenges to ongoing love relationships, in terms of core personality conflicts which have to be reconciled and balanced out in the context of the whole relationship. It's vital not to focus on differences and magnify them, it's more important to see the overall good the relationship delivers to you both, and work from there.

Career and Aspiration

Gemini could be avoiding responsibility for your actions or focusing strongly on certain aspects of your job or business while pushing the more difficult tasks to the back burner, or even denying they exist.

You could have recently made a decision that was based on your desire for popularity, acceptance or social importance and yet the results were not what you expected. You're inclined to blame others for misleading you, but in truth everyone was playing a game that you got caught up in.

All recent discussions and new business relationships must be reviewed, perhaps some served a purpose, but it's clear that not all can go into the future.

During this phase, it is important not to be controversial, it's better to keep your head down, work hard and do what is required with the minimum of fuss.

It is also an important time to eliminate what is unnecessary in your life, so you shouldn't take on extra work if it's tangential, and it's not necessarily a good month to take on a very large client. If you are offered a big contract, you should be very careful of the obligations, the work schedule and the commitment required, because it may be very enticing financially, but it could be terrible for your health and work life balance, so think carefully before taking on anything big.

Excitement and Motivation

The home sphere is central to fun and fulfilment and Gemini can enjoy doing home improvements or buying things for the home that will enhance your ability to relax or entertain.

You can however bite off more than you can chew as the expectations are high and not everything goes as planned, but that should not deter you from trying to bring some vision to the home environment.

The satisfaction you get from your home or private space could be less active and more subtle, in that you may enjoy researching something or immersing yourself in reading and escaping, via literature, into a different perspective or bubble.

Home and family life are often a welcome distraction from business responsibilities, and it's often easier for you to strike a healthy balance between your home and business responsibilities and work.

Marriage and Family

In July there are both inner and outer conflicts that Gemini is grappling with. There is some disharmony which can make daily life difficult and could be putting pressure on your marriage. You should take time to think about why you're so self-critical right now and where exactly your guilt stems from, often something has triggered these feelings and yet it's a good time to acknowledge them and then for your to tackle them.

Gemini should also think about your personal needs, priorities and your underlying beliefs to ensure that they are in tune with how you are conducting your relationships - are you actually living a lie? Is that where the guilt stems from?

Less authentic and forthcoming communication could also lead to doubt about each other's motives in love. The foundation for your relationship feels less clear and that's creating ambivalent emotions between you and your partner.

Money and Finance

This month there is conflict over money in business and love because the priorities of Gemini are not compatible with those people you have to make decisions with.

It may be more difficult to get a loan or a bank manager may get on your back with more stringent demands.

This may be a month where a mortgage or fixed rate deals to be negotiated, and that can be quite a convoluted task as there will be a minefield of new information to explore.

Gemini may feel a little powerless, you have to be patient in financial dealings as it's not simple to reach agreement or find easy solutions.

Living and Loving to the Full

True magic in love this month comes from appreciation of how a relationship makes you feel at a deep level and by moving away from superficial, short term remedies or conversations.

To develop a strong bond, or deepen the bond, you and your partner may need to weather a few storms together and so some challenges should be seen as creative opportunities to explore more deeply the connection.

If your partnership is not deeply rewarding or satisfying, this month will expose the fact that perhaps you and a partner don't have a powerful attraction. A desire to sail through the storms together can indicate an innate connection that's leading to fulfilment down the line.

Planetary Cautions

This is not a good time to challenge authority or to stick your neck out. It's probably best to play it safe and avoid unnecessary publicity.

This is not an ideal time for public speaking and very high profile events in general.

Responsibilities you have should be acknowledged and not avoided this is not a time for short cuts and bending the rules.

When conflicts arise with your parents or your boss, you should seek to clarify their demands and reflect on how to tackle the issue carefully rather than getting drawn into anything heated.

Moon Magic

The new moon phase extends from the 17th of July to the 30th of July this waxing phase is the perfect fortnight for new initiatives, setting plans, establishing goals, starting anything prospective and being proactive. This is the action phase, details below:

On the 23rd Venus goes retrograde in Leo, this indicates that internet and cyber dating is not favored from this date. Negotiations and business discussions are protracted. This is not the best time for strenuous exercise, strict routines and confrontation. It's not a great time for business trips.

Not a great time for IT projects. Internet dating is not favored. Negotiations may be fruitless. Not the best time for short distance travel.

Applying for loans and debt is not favored. Not a good period for new tax arrangements. Sex therapy is not favored.

An excellent time for family events, entertaining and dinner parties. Catering and hospitality businesses are favored.

AUGUST

Energies and Essence: "Reach for the stars, follow your heart's desire."

This is a time where you need to double down on your career, if you are chasing ambitions you should be secure in your knowledge, in your experience and in the direction you are taking, but you should also be willing to learn and to adjust. This is a time to seize opportunities, and it's also a time of great equilibrium as your career and home life should both be proceeding quite smoothly.

It's important right now to be cognizant of the greater good and you need to operate with an awareness of your own journey, but also the way you're interacting with other people who are also experiencing a journey. Try not to see everything as competitive, rather seize the chance to help everyone else, no matter where they are on their journey, and it's very important to be non-judgmental and to have a very broad minded attitude when it comes to different perspectives and opinions.

Affirmation: "I am confident in my future aims and I'm reaching for the stars, but always with benevolence."

Love and Romance

Ideally, love relationships are an escape from the stresses and strains of the world this month. A positive new relationship provides real soul food and some spiritual guidance to Gemini. Love and romance should be a refuse and an arena where you acquire solace.

However, the energies this month tend to pierce through that veil of self-defense and Gemini may have to come to terms with any self-doubts and perpetual suspicions about the opposite sex that serve to undermine true emotional rapport. The more you carry around negative self-talk about relationships, trust and intimacy, the less you can benefit from a relationship this month and the more you're prone to manipulation.

However, you also have a chance to realize whatever it is that's always leading your relationships into trouble, and the ways you often self-sabotages or shuts down emotionally making a partner feel neglected or distant.

This month can serve as a wake-up call to keep things in better perspective in love and prevent self-doubt leading to self-sabotage.

Career and Aspiration

This is an excellent time for creativity, brainstorming and coming up with novel ideas to enhance your business or to improve client relations. It's very important for you to keep track of everything that's going on and keep a list of names and contact details. Good admin and managing client email lists is extremely important, simply because you are likely to be deluged with enquiries and interest in your products.

You tend to feel rather positively inspired and pretty much everything seems like a great idea, but it's important for you to be able to assess things in a more logical way for longer term potential and pitfalls. This month is certainly a good one for creating opportunities, enhancing networking and finding new suppliers or important information, but it's not a great time for concrete and definite financial decisions that will have long-term consequences. August is far better for shorter term marketing and promotional goals, because you are not adequately reflective or focused to make good decisions for long-term business or management decisions.

Even though the focus is on outer development and achievement, this is also a fantastic time to get in touch with your inner feelings. Often things that happen as you pursue your career or interact with people in power or colleagues, have important lessons which reflect on you as a person. You are more able, because of your confidence, to face the inner aspects of yourself that you might have been a little bit afraid to acknowledge, or to reflect on before.

Excitement and Motivation

This is a very stimulating month and it is possible for Gemini to make new discoveries and encounter different people which will be quite fascinating.

There tends to be a lot of information and new experiences coming your way, which can help you in a business sense, in terms of hobbies or signify promise romantically.

However, there can also be a lot of confusion and raised expectations, therefore it's very important for you to keep your emotions in check and take a wait-and-see attitude before ploughing in head long.

This is an exciting yet nerve-racking month, simply because the pace is quite relentless. It's busy on a social front and it can be busy at work too, particularly if you are involved in a career that involves people. Not all the plans you make will work out, it's rather a white knuckle ride but there's no shortage of opportunity and excitement.

Marriage and Family

This month circumstances within the relationship or events that occur to Gemini and your partner can provide greater clarity on parts of the relationship where you are both selfish or fail to recognize each other's needs.

It's a month to be aware of relationship blind spots, these are the issues or situations in a relationship where you feel you're doing your best and not being appreciated, but where your partner feels you're failing to listen and properly engage.

In relationships, it's so easy for both parties to subjectivity 'rate their performance' rather than paying attention to the cues their partner is giving them. We are all subjectively predisposed to illusions about ourselves and our behavior, but the key in love this month is for Gemini to understand the reality of how you and your partner actually respond to each other's needs, desires and cries for help. Then to start proactively probing what the unmet needs and emotional cravings in the relationship and to deal with that.

Money and Finance

This month Gemini can be quite idealistic in the way you spend money. It's important for you to be cautious when investing in activities or ventures that claim to be charitable and humanitarian, as they may not be.

There could be some disappointment in terms of assets or equipment you've recently invested in and if you do go ahead with a purchase this month you should ensure you have adequate guarantees or warranties.

It's often wise for you to be cautious in your dealings with bureaucracies or large corporations because it can be very hard to get fair treatment and you may bound up in red tape for lengthy periods. It's a month when it's hard to get seen as an individual with specific needs when dealing with a bank or trying to manage a contract with a large organization or government department.

Living and Loving to the Full

In order to enhance love magic this month, Gemini need a lot of variety and choice. You've got ants in your pants and your restless nature is stirred meaning you need lots of novelty and the stimulus of new ideas, venues or activities.

You are inspired by a very active social life, or by taking short trips away. This is actually an excellent month of the year for travel and for experiencing different cultures and geographical locations, so in order to inspire passion in your love relationship, it's a very good idea to get away from anything routine and humdrum.

It's also great to get away from the hassle of home life, the neighborhood or your respective parents for a break.

Planetary Cautions

Mercury goes retrograde on the 24th in Virgo, indicating that large family events or trips as a family are not favored after that time.

Property deals and making contracts for home improvements are also not advisable after this date.

You should exercise caution when handling machinery or tools as to avoid accidents in the home.

Mercury goes retrograde conjunct Mars indicating that you can be quite hot-headed and tempers can flare in the family front making this is a different time to achieve harmony and cooperation.

This is definitely not a good time to invite people or relatives to stay.

Moon Magic

The new moon phase extends from the 16th of August to the 30th of August this waxing phase is the perfect fortnight for new initiatives, setting plans, establishing goals, starting anything prospective and being proactive. This is the action phase, details below:

Financial affairs, new business and sales volume are favored. A good time for investing and buying assets for a business. A great time for a promotion or increase.

Not an ideal time for totally new activities or vigorous physical exercise. Dental work is not favored. Sporting competitive events are also not ideal. Not a great time for leadership.

Property matters and home improvements are not favored.

New romance and dating are very successful.
Excellent time for marriage. Long haul travel is favored.

New business partnerships are successful. A good time to get advice.

Personal development and spiritual growth are favored.

Not a good time for PR, public speaking or challenging authority.

SEPTEMBER

Energies and Essence: "Ca sera sera!"

This month Jupiter turns retrograde in Taurus and the key is not to tempt fate. You must seek acceptance and resolution.

It's important to understand that what's meant to be is meant to be, and some things aren't meant to be l. It's also important to remember that all good things come to an end, life is a series of cycles and there are r ups and downs as well as ebbs and flows and sometimes we need to go with those and not fight against them. Astrology of course is all about being proactive and working with the planetary energies, it's very important always be proactive and positive in everything you do, but it's also important to understand timing and to know when the time is right.

True wisdom is understanding that everything has its time and has its purpose, and sometimes when the purpose has been exhausted, it's time to let go and embrace something new.

Affirmation: "I appreciate what every experience in life has taught me, but I release these and let them go."

Love and Romance

This is a busy and quite taxing month in romance, you will have to work harder at your love life simply because the demands of love relationships are more stringent during this phase. It's important to have good discussions, to strive for justice in love and to be able to stand up for yourself and get your demands and needs met.

It's highly possible that a new relationship can get off the ground very quickly, however it may be quite an impetuous relationship and tempers may flair.

New romances can be fast paced, very exciting and highly stimulating.

If your love life had been particularly dull, this is a great time to spice things up and get things moving in the right direction again.

Communication in relationships is enhanced favoring internet dating and long distance relationships.

Career and Aspiration

The root of many issues this September is actually your own preconceived ideas, these often stem from unacknowledged fears about leadership, taking a stand and being wrong. It's important for you to understand your own motivations in terms of your career, as this will help bring your clarity about what you will , and will not stand for.

It's a time of understanding what drew your to the current position you are in career wise, are you fulfilling the goals or objectives you believe you would. If the answer is no, you need to begin thinking long term about a career move. It's about getting back to basics and getting back together what you intended when you set out on a certain path before things got in the way.

Excitement and Motivation

This month your energy is quite focused and you have the resolve to complete what is needed for you to make progress on your important goals.

You can access a determination, focus and the ability to stick with a particular task no matter how boring it may seem. Often, you can derive great satisfaction and even enjoyment by delving into the detail of something and perhaps uncovering a mystery. You're looking for anything that's hidden and in that you can become very engrossed.

As Mars enters Libra, this signifies an excellent month for sporting and competitive activities where you can enjoy physical activity and contact sports.

This is also a fun time for you to work with children training them, coaching or teaching them.

Marriage and Family

It's important for Gemini not to be too narrow in your thinking when it comes to solutions in love. While knowing the difference between right and wrong, reality and fantasy, fact and fiction is important; it's still important for you to acknowledge grey areas and nuance. Nothing can be gained by attempting to box everything into a category or reduce complex problems to simple solutions.

There's more scope and greater possibilities right now than you currently realize and so there's much to be gained even if you feel a little flat.

This month marks a turning point in terms of communication. It's been a busy year, there's been some passion and some problems to be worked through. You were required to be more assertive in love and to set boundaries or address power balance in the relationship, but now is a time for healing, forgiveness and harmony. So it's important to pursue activities that are conducive to the emotional and spiritual well-being of you both. This is a time when it's easier to reach agreement, there are fewer pressing dilemmas and hurdles, and that's why you both begin to feel a little bit relaxed and even things over which you have clashed can be resolved.

It's important for your not to dwell, as often this means you're looking at too narrow a part of the picture.

If you're spending extra time at work, that could indicate a certain amount of avoidant behavior towards relationships, however the distraction of work can often help you to avoid dwelling and getting fixated on one issue.

Money and Finance

This is an excellent time for business and scenario planning. It's ideal for doing ROI, return on investment calculations and looking at plan B and C's.

As you're in quite a conservative frame of mind, yet are also quite creative, this is a very good month for solid planning for the months ahead.

This is a very good month for Gemini in graphic design, website design and social media marketing, but solid market research is vital to avoid a mismatch between the site design or social media strategy.

Customer service and a strong focus on building a good reputation is vital.

Living and Loving to the Full

With Venus going direct in Leo from the 4th, this is an excellent time to set up a dating app profile or to be more active on social media in general as a way of you meeting new potential partners.

You should take advantage of work socials and trips away with colleagues, as these could lead to romance.

In existing relationships, laughter is the best medicine! Humor and fun are vital in September and you and a partner should think more about the fun side of the relationship. What used to make you guys laugh? What made you feel light-hearted? It's time to get away from negativity and work related conversation and find your 'funny bones ' again by doing life enhancing activities that make you s laugh. It's important to avoid conversations or activities that bring you both down unnecessary and rather choose activities that are uplifting in some way.

Planetary Cautions

Mercury is retrograde in Virgo until the 16th and it turns direct opposite Saturn in Pisces.

Until the 16th is not a good time for property matters or renovations. Family issues could remain unresolved and it's not a great time for family events or entertaining.

Projects connected to research are not favored.

This likely to be a month of contraction where certain aspects of your life grind to a halt or experience more push back especially from authority figures. However, instead of being frustrated, it's an ideal time to review rules, laws and protocols and get clarity before things pick up in pace again.

It's important not to avoid problems at the moment, but at the same time you should not seek quick solutions as these are often just sticking plaster.

This is a time of slightly cautious or pessimistic thinking and thus it's not ideal for public debate or being highly visible in your career. It is however an excellent time for deeper understanding and diligent preparation for the rest of the year.

Moon Magic

The new moon phase extends from the 14th of September to the 29th of September, this waxing phase is the perfect fortnight for new initiatives, setting plans, establishing goals, starting anything prospective and being proactive. This is the action phase, details below:

This may be a tricky time for new contracts and negotiations. Financial matters need additional information and research.

Business travel maybe a waste of time.

An excellent waxing period for new relationships, dating, romance and getting married or engaged. Matters pertaining to children are favored.

This is ideal for creative and artistic ventures as well as arts management.

Legal affairs are successful.

OCTOBER

Energies and Essence: "But giving into the nighttime
Ain't no cure for the pain
You gotta wade into the water
You gotta learn to live again."

This is a time where you feel more energized, health and vitality are stronger but you should also focus on preventative measures to protect your health. So this is a really good time to arrest any bad habits, it's an important time to have wellness goals and these should include putting aside time for fun, enjoyment, positive interaction with other people, affection and also good health.

They say people who suffer ill health often don't get enough hugs, and while 'm not quite sure how scientific that is, but this month to draw strength from positive and loving relationships, be they friendship bonds, marital bonds, family bonds and that means making sure you give hugs, receive hugs and are tactile with those closest to you. There's an interchange of positive energy when you react physically with others.

Alternatively you must keep your aura clear by staying away from bitter and twisted toxic people.

Affirmation: "I know my thoughts affect my well-being, I chose to have thoughts that enhance my health and I welcome positive interaction with others."

Love and Romance

Physical attraction plays a large role in new love as does adventure and taboo breaking. New relationships are exciting but quite nerve wracking as they threaten to disrupt both your status quo and your perceptions of life.

Gemini should be ready for a love affair that will rewrite your rules and your script for your life, as this new partner could shake up your priorities in ways you don't expect.

This is a very good month for new romances; your love life tends to be fuel injected and you may feel the thrust like the G force when a plane takes off as you meet a potential new beau. The relationship may not head for full blown dating right away, there may be a period of cat and mouse as you guys feel each other out and play a somewhat of a role, leaving getting to know each other properly for later.

Career and Aspiration

It's a great month for activities that require a great deal of daring and even ruthlessness. Gemini have your eye on the prize, you're uncompromising and ready to do what it takes to achieve your goals.

You have to be a little cautious as it's not necessarily a great month for extreme sports or highly risky physical activities.

The strength of your convictions is often the make or break factor in terms of getting results in your workplace.

You're perfectionistic and often this month the fixated, work a holic side of your nature kicks in. You know how to drive home an advantage, however you're often oblivious to the concerns of those around you.

You're often dogmatic which is unusual for Gemini, and you've not got a reverse gear.

It's very important for you not to ignore the spiritual wisdom available. Don't let your inner voice be drowned out by constant distractions and preoccupation, the key phrase for this month is: "there's nothing to fear but fear itself." This is a time to harness your emotions and desires in order to conquer your fears, never lose trust in yourself and what you're doing.

This is an important time to take responsibility and show mastery over your life, it is important not to let the small things get the better of you. Often during this phase there are hurdles, and yes you have to acknowledge there are fears and weaknesses to be overcome, but the best way to deal with these is not by acting impulsively, irrationally or getting angry, you have to harness all that anger and turn it into power.

Excitement and Motivation

This is a time when leadership is successful and you can make a splash. It's a good time for new activities and ventures involving leisure and entertainment.

You come out on top when you stick to your guns and follow through with determination, despite the odds

The eclipse brings strength and vitality to Gemini, and you feel luck is on your side, and so it's a good time to make a move romantically or launch a creative project. There is increased joy and happiness available if you grab opportunities quickly.

Because you achieve more personal fulfillment this month, you can provide others with inspiration and support. People will be drawn to you because they perceive the warm and vibrant energy which you exude, this makes you a very effective leader.

Your sense of confidence means that the law of attraction operates strongly, but you should be careful of what you wish for.

Things are likely to go your way and if they don't, you'll certainly find a way of snatching a last minute gain.

Marriage and Family

You may have to be careful of being pushy with your children and possibly arguing with your partner about how to bring up the children.

Gemini are after security in marriage and long term relationships this year, and that can bring out a controlling streak not usually prevalent in Gemini in October. This month you can be quite prescriptive, fussy or pedantic and often this is about control. A sudden tendency to fault find or be critical can reveal insecurities and a slight projection.

Gemini are eager for greater influence in all that you and others do, and thus you may seem overbearing in relationships and family decisions, as you can insist on your way or the high way.

It's not a good month for your partner to test you by flirting as you're often quite jealous.

You're more amorous in love, your desire level is high - well-handled you can be an excellent lover who is more passionate and amorous, however you could become hostile and argumentative due to jealousy and frustration at lack of attention from your partner.

Money

This month you need to be cautious of borrowing money for speculative ventures.

You must also be more reticent about taking leadership roles in managing large amounts of money as you may not understand all the agendas at play.

Issues connected to tax, audit and new investments must be undertaken with caution.

This is an excellent month for projects involving science, technology, research and development.

You should be cautious in accepting tips or donations that are too generous.

Living and Loving to the Full

With the eclipse in Libra, and Mars and Mercury spending time in Libra this month, this is an excellent time for you to be proactive and optimistic about your love life.

It's a time when you win in love when you show generosity of spirit and are supportive to your partner.

Relationships where Gemini and your partner cheer each other on and are mutually supportive are much more successful.

It's important not to be jealous or competitive, you should understand that when your partner grows as a person through success or self-expression, it makes the relationship stronger not weaker.

Planetary Cautions

This is not the best month to take on debt or begin a joint venture.

It's also a time to be careful of misinformation from people you trust.

There may be errors of omission or commission and it's important for you to do your own research and remain skeptical as others may be concealing things from you.

This is still a month to be cautious of extreme sports.

You should be careful of being ensnared by so called 'good' causes that aren't good.

Moon Magic

The new moon phase extends from the 14th of October to the 30th of October, this waxing phase is the perfect fortnight for new initiatives, setting plans, establishing goals, starting anything prospective and being proactive. This is the action phase, details below:

Financial matters are more important and critical and need greater focus.

A time of intense work and important decisions about work. Negotiations are more vital.

Promotions, advertising and publishing are favored. Good for long haul travel. International trade is successful. Good for academic goals.

NOVEMBER

Energies and Essence: "Banging your own drum."

The key right now, is never say never! Remain open minded and stay on your toes ready to explore and experience new things.

This is not a time to follow the crowd, it's also not a time when you should be concerned about fitting in or pleasing other people. The truth is what you should focus on, as without truth, nothing leads anywhere, and so it's up to you to follow whatever unusual path you consider necessary in order to find the truth, and you should let both facts, new techniques and intuition lead you on that path.

It's important not to count anything out, and it's also not important not to be swept along with the crowd. Remember, just because everyone is doing or saying something is no guarantee that they know what they are doing or talking about.

Affirmation: "I trust in my unique ideas and instincts and I'm confident in following my unique path.

Love and Romance

What happens in love and romance this month has greater significance and intensity that usual and can stir up some powerful emotions both good and bad. Emotions tend rush to the surface, some heavy some passionate and yet none easy to ignore. While relationships which start now may not last; they can be triggers for a revolution in your life and a deeper connection with yourself.

Even stable romantic relationships cut deeper and demand changes and evolvement from your, perhaps more so than of your partner.

The only downside this month is Gemini are impatient with problems – so are likely to gloss over any issues your partner may have and sweep them away for another day, "Don't rain on my parade" kinda thing. I think you should try to be diplomatic, i.e., where you express that perhaps this is not the time for major discussions due to the fact you're in a light-hearted mood and don't want to be brought down, but you should take note and you should make time for a much more heartfelt deep and meaningful debate or confrontation later.

Career and Aspiration

You have a desire to release yourself from the restrictions of your life and daily routine. You may find a sudden excuse for release from a limiting place in your life such as a job, a business relationship, or a way of life. You are more excitable, and you want to spice up your life in any way possible.

You may feel as though this 'breaking away' is a great relief. However, it is important not to throw away worthwhile things in your life for the sake of freedom but to figure out carefully what things are no longer needed in your life.

November is excellent for decisions and new beginnings, sometimes they are planned, sometimes fate plays a role, and yet in both cases the changes seem to be pre-ordained and there is a strong force propelling your forward like it's meant to be.

You can be obsessive and dogmatic and this is not a good time for team work as you're so self-motivated and quite arrogant, you shun advice and you're convinced you know best.

Excitement and Motivation

It's time for your to take a chance grab an opportunity to develop your skills or expand your level of experience.

You may almost feel divinely inspired, like you have the truth on your side and nothing can stop you.

Interactions with co-workers can be stimulating, entertaining and also distracting, and so you need to keep focus on your objectives. Work-related issues can become blurred where it is not clear where your responsibilities end and another's begin, and you may feel you're doing more than your fair share – this probably means you're the more capable and organized one, but you should not let it lead to stress and overwork.

In some cases a new person is willing to coach and mentor you along the way to help you get where you want.

It's quite a surprising period, however you must ensure that you retain your dignity during this month, as it's easy to lose control and be little self-centered.

You may have fun working with a charitable organization or providing your services to a not-for-profit to help those in need.

Marriage and Family

Marriage relations improve as you are open to listening and are more understanding of your partner's points of view, you're ready to take new information on board and can do so objectively. You are less inclined to get emotional or become defensive, as you can see the logic of what your partner is conveying. However, you will not hold back on your own opinions either, and you can be tempted to take the moral high ground and assume a righteous approach.

The key is to be positive and think of solutions, trying not to get sidetracked into the rights and wrongs, not everything had a moral angle to it. This is a very good time for Gemini to plan with your partner and set goals for your future. You have a greater need to know where the relationship is going, and so you won't sit back and let it drift along. If things have been strained, this is an excellent time to restore communication, trust and start building up again rather than breaking down.

Money and Finances

Important conversations about money, priorities and fundamental problems or conflicts at the heart of the relationship need to be broached. This is a chance to renew and redirect the relationship with some fresh understanding. However, success in discussions depends on how mature you both are, and also how genuinely willing you both are to understand each other, acknowledge the problems and see it from each other's point of view.

It can be a very fruitful time where a depth of understanding can be achieved, however if there is a fundamental lack of compatibility, then your partner may obfuscate or refuse to talk honestly. Gemini is likely to have greater problems reaching some form of resolution with partners from the cardinal and even more, the mutable signs on money issues.

Living and Loving to the Full

This is an excellent month for your to let your hair down in terms of dating, someone may offer to set you up on a blind date or introduce you to one of their single friends and you shouldn't balk, you should take a gamble.

When it comes to love, even though you may feel as though you're being silly or juvenile, something from left field may turn out to be a great way to meeting someone special.

Planetary Cautions

You have to be careful of team related activities as you can get quite frustrated and angry in this environment and may end up feeling it was all a waste of time.

It's not the best month for health and fitness goals and you should be careful with medication and natural supplements. It's wise to stick with what you know rather than trying any newfangled or unrested solutions to health issues.

Moon Magic

The new moon phase extends from the 13th of November to the 27th of November, this waxing phase is the perfect fortnight for new initiatives, setting plans, establishing goals, starting anything prospective and being proactive. This is the action phase, details below:

Financial matters and negotiation are not favored. Short and long distance travel, business travel and new long distance love is not favored. Not a good time for large scale purchases. Not a good time for a new learning course.

Publishing, academic matters, advertising and international trade aren't favored.

Energies and Essence: To taste the sweet
I face the pain
I rise and fall

Yet through it all
This much remains
I want one moment in time
When I'm more than I thought I could be."

Some of the inner battles you face are the toughest, and yes, in many cases, these are inner battles even if they appear to be a struggle against authority or a person. Someone only has as much power over you as you give them – if you back down, they take more of your power away. This month is not so much about striking out as chipping away at that power – that hold they have over you until you have enough confidence to make that break and take back control. Do not project your problems onto the outer world; look within for the answers and ask yourself what is it about you that allows these forces to control you. Small steps that rebuild your belief in yourself and your own power, soon amount to something quite significant.

Affirmation: "I am in control of myself and my fate and others or circumstances can only stand in my way if I allow."

Love and Romance

While single Gemini are rather open-minded and adventurous in love, you are not reckless, and while you may experiment socially and on the dating scene, you will actually be slow to commit regarding feelings. You will gravitate to wiser and possibly older potential lovers as you are seeking not just companionship but all-round expansion in terms of love, and that can mean intellectual and spiritual. You will look to grow from the experiences of your partner, and this can mean that in marriages and new love affairs, your partner will have valuable advice and guidance to share with you. This can help you in a practical and also a spiritual way.

Confusion and intense situations hanging over from last month will continue to disturb your inner peace; it can be hard to switch off from the issues that are going on around you and relax. It is very important this month for you to find an inner space that feels safe. You need either a physical or mental outlet which allows you to escape from the emotional environment around you.

Career and Aspiration

This month is both disruptive and dynamic in work. You may feel that you have been thrown into the deep end and have to make decisions based on very little information. It can be an exciting time at work as events are fast-paced, and there is much novelty and innovation regarding new systems, new training, new staff and new premises, and while things may be up in the air, it is more interesting.

December is excellent for those Gemini s who work in fast-paced industries, i.e., technology, media, advertising, politics or banking – any work where events in the outside world can inject new information which speeds things and forces you to change course. If you're looking for a new job, this month is ideal in terms of there being many prospects, although it can be very confusing regarding making a clear choice between options, and so if you do take on a new position, you may be a little in the dark as to what your job description is – you may have quite a bit of autonomy in the new role and be able to make it your own. Opportunities can arise at work quite unexpectedly, and you will be up for the challenges.

Excitement and Motivation

This month is one when your imagination is on fire, and the creative juices are flowing. Energy is behind your creative process, and you can productively transfer ideas and imagery into concrete form. Music production, placing lyrics to music and also arranging music is something you can be very effective with. There is a great appreciation of the more subtle concepts in art and music, and you are inspired and moved emotionally by art forms. You may visit art galleries or go on excursions with others where you s visit cultural places of interest and write about or discuss this.

This is also a good time to collaborate with others or support others with the same creative interests. This is a month filled with distractions, and you may not make much concrete progress regarding goals – you will, however, gain valuable insights and encouraging support for your ideas. This month is ideal for brainstorming, visualizing goals and outcomes and thinking up a range of creative approaches – there are many ways to skin a cat.

Marriage and Family

Love life is both energetic and also contentious. You can be rather snappy and also aggressive regarding how you project – yes, you're a little bossy and perhaps not in the mood to listen properly. You do need to pause and take time to at least consider the opinions of your partner as you're likely to dismiss them out of hand and take a 'my way or the highway' attitude.

On a positive note, you can be very helpful in terms of assisting your loved one with tasks, problems or their family – there is a fine line between offering help and taking over and so you need to know when to help and when to take a step back.

You're the initiator in December regarding sex life as you will have loads of energy to spare and are feeling more amorous than usual. No matter how your partner is feeling, you will drag them along with you and make sure you inject them with your enthusiasm.

Money and Finance

Mercury goes retrograde on the 12th in your solar eighth house. This poses difficulties for the household finances and if you s are married or share a bank account, there can be disagreements or discord about how and where money is spent. The retrograde period indicates that debt, taxes and issues about money are top of the agenda and often recent decisions have to be scrutinized or reassessed. It's also possible that you s will blame each other for the outcome of recent financial decisions as there is a tendency to pass the buck until the dust settles and a plan is put in place.

Living and Loving to the Full

There is a strong element of returning karma to this month – good deeds done can result in assistance coming at an opportune time. However, if you have been a recipient of a good deed, it is now time for you to pay that favor back – either way it should be a positive experience of mutual cooperation. This month is one where a moment in time or a shared experience no matter how brief can tie your destiny to another for a long time.

Planetary Cautions

In many relationships, what pulls you and your partner together and what you have in common can actually be part of the problem. For example, if you work in the same company, you may find yourself on different sides of an argument or issue, and this may create conflict. Even if you share religious vies, you may differ on a specific issue and that may drive a wedge. Issues with family, for example, where one of your relatives is always clashing with one of your partner's, making family events awkward or impossible, can come to a head. Home life can be strained, and many unimportant issues can become flashpoints, just because you need to let off steam. Taking yourselves too seriously is the biggest problem – you and your partner need to be more relaxed, more flexible, and more patient.

You are more sensitive to criticism and may feel that people are working at cross-purposes to your goals. Confrontations are more likely as you are unwilling to engage in any compromise if it threatens your own agenda. This is obviously not the best time to enter into negotiations where you have more to lose by being difficult or stubborn, as other people will be more defensive when they feel the sheer force of your personal power. In its most positive form this time may signal the beginning of a new partnership, but you're likely to attract someone who stands up to you or pushes you to achieve more, and relationships now will seem more competitive. Have more confidence in your own abilities and avoid feeling threatened by other people who have different opinions.

Moon Magic

The new moon phase extends from the 12th of December to the 26th of December, this waxing phase is the perfect fortnight for new initiatives, setting plans, establishing goals, starting anything prospective and being proactive. This is the action phase, details below:

Caution is needed in financial matters and negotiation. Business trips aren't favored.

Mercury retrograde in Capricorn on the 13th indicates problems getting financing or loans. Dealing with banks is more difficult. Tax matters are complicated.

Good for marriage and engagement. Excellent for new relationships and dating. Spiritual growth and self-development are successful. Good for retreats, romance and musical events. Excellent for creative matters.

Well that's a wrap of our biggest most comprehensive Gemini Horoscope yet.

Whether you are a Gemini or know a Gemini, I do believe you will have found this very helpful and informative.

I aim to give you a variety of advice based on psychology, spiritual insight, relationship advice and business guidance, so you get a little bit of everything.

Take care and have a wonderful 2023.

Blessings, Lisa.

Printed in Great Britain
by Amazon

18547896R00058